WE ARE MONKEYS

HAPPY WITH WHO WE ARE

By Juhi Nachane

DEDICATION

For Parth and Meera, my favourite storytellers.

I love you both to the moon and back.

Special thanks to Himanshu

for always being there when I needed him.

Last but not the least, thank you to my loving parents for

their endless love, support and encouragement.

First paperback edition September 2023

Illustrated by Shey Kolee

ISBN: 979-8-89109-067-5 (paperback)
ISBN: 979-8-89109-689-9 (hardcover)
ISBN: 979-8-89109-068-2 (ebook)

Visit author website at www.tinytaletown.com.

Mommy monkey, Daddy monkey, their son Philly,
and their daughter Milly lived in the jungles of Jim Corbett,
a national park in northern India.

Philly and Milly would roam around the jungle,

searching for unusual things humans had left behind.

They always found a use for these unusual things.

They used an umbrella to store rainwater.

They used torn bags to build a hammock for a swing.

They used a torch to make shadows and scare neighboring animals at night.

They used a spoon and ladle to play beautiful music and dance around.

10

One day while finding food with their daddy in the jungle, they saw a man and a woman trying to set up a tent and beside was a big bag of things.

Philly turned to Milly. "Are these humans? Why do they have so many things, and why have they covered themselves? It is so, so hot!!"

Milly whispered, "They are our distant cousins. Mommy told me. They don't have tails, are scared of climbing trees, and don't jump and swing. And they always cover themselves."

"Whaaat . . . Cousins?? Without tails and scared of climbing trees? Now that's simply hilarious." Philly laughed.

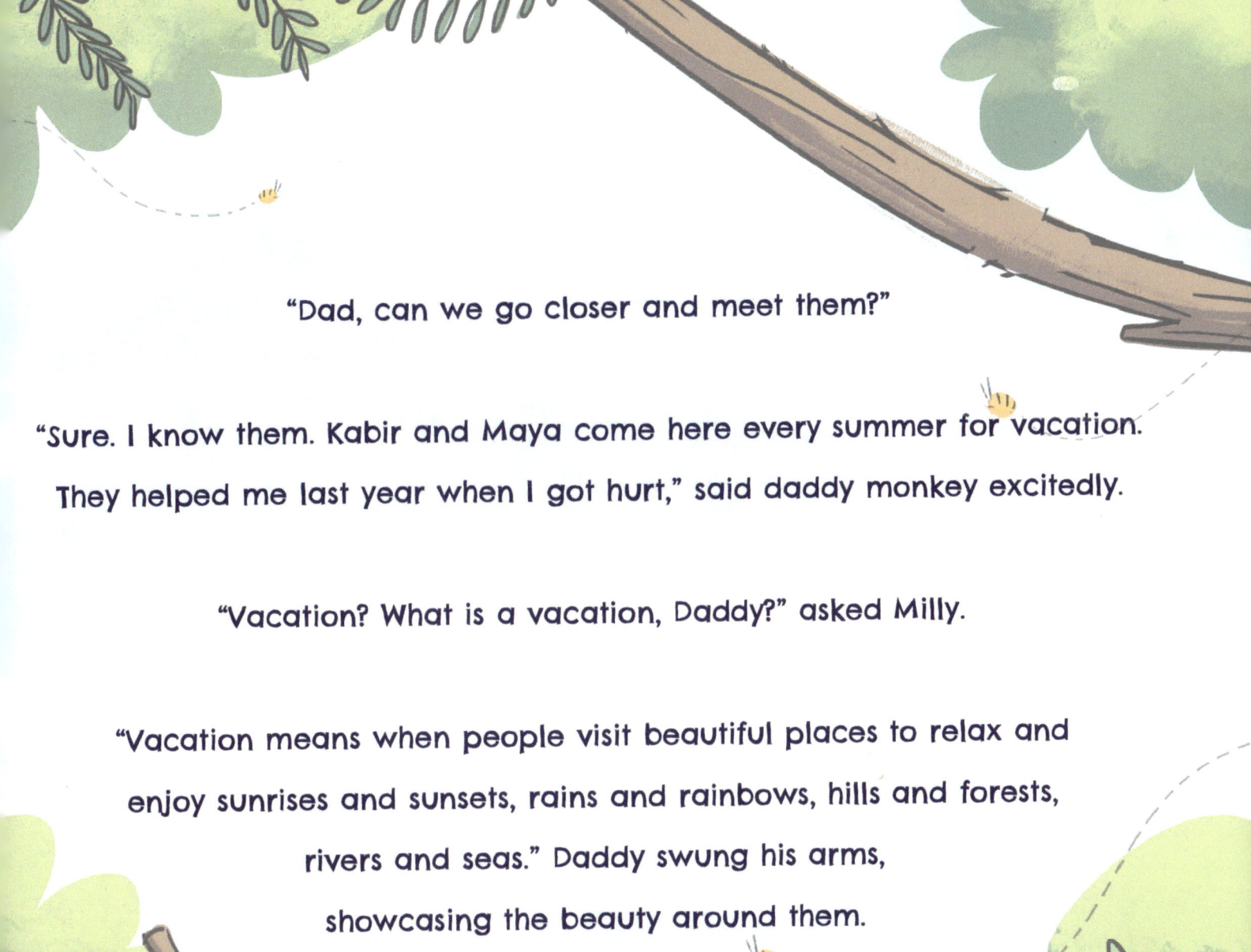

"Dad, can we go closer and meet them?"

"Sure. I know them. Kabir and Maya come here every summer for vacation. They helped me last year when I got hurt," said daddy monkey excitedly.

"Vacation? What is a vacation, Daddy?" asked Milly.

"Vacation means when people visit beautiful places to relax and enjoy sunrises and sunsets, rains and rainbows, hills and forests, rivers and seas." Daddy swung his arms, showcasing the beauty around them. "I'll introduce you."

14

When the monkeys approached Kabir and Maya,
the humans smiled, recognizing Daddy.

"Are these your kids? They are so lovely," said Kabir.

He and Maya stretched their hands and
asked Philly and Milly to come closer.
Philly and Milly looked at their father and
climbed up on the humans' shoulders.

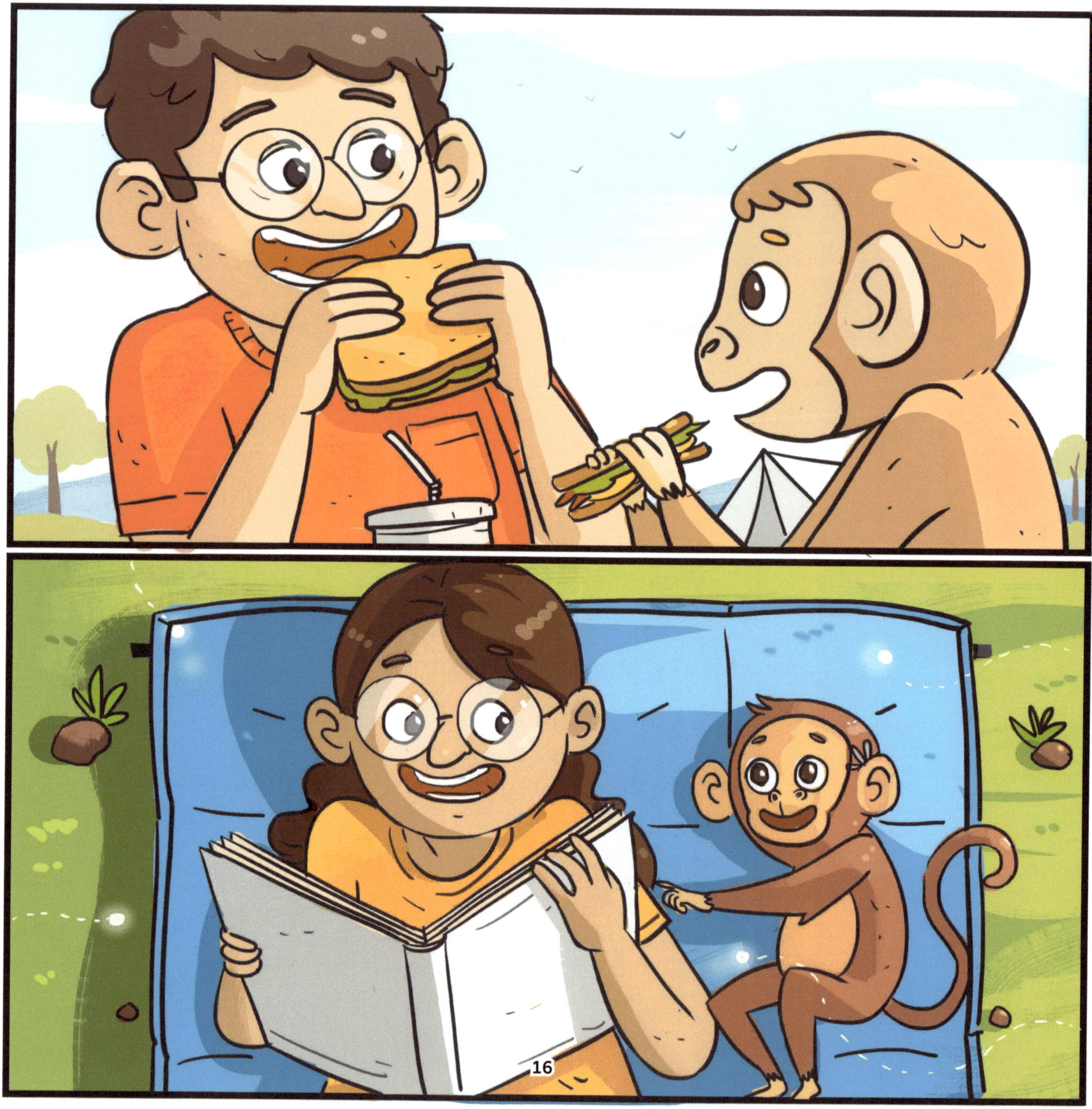

They happily roamed around with their cousins,

enjoyed their food,

drank some orange juice,

and took an afternoon nap on their camping beds.

When they returned home, they told their mommy about their day. Just as they were about to go to sleep in their home tree, Philly said, "I wish I was like Kabir. I could sleep on a comfortable bed."

"Yes, I wish I was beautiful like Maya," said Milly.

Mommy monkey said, "Philly, you always loved your sleeping branch. What changed after meeting Kabir and Maya?"

Daddy monkey hugged Milly and said, "Milly, you are a beautiful monkey, my princess. You can never be happy if you compare yourself with others."

The next morning, Mommy woke up Philly and Milly.

"Come on, my little monkeys. We need to go find some food."

Philly sighed. "Not bananas again. I wish I was Kabir.
I could have some refreshing orange juice."

Daddy said, "We can eat oranges in the winter, Philly.
Why don't you splash some water from your umbrella?
That will be refreshing."

"Daddy, umbrellas are not for storing water.
I was stupid. They're for protecting us from the rain so we don't get wet.
Kabir and Maya are so smart and cool," said Philly.

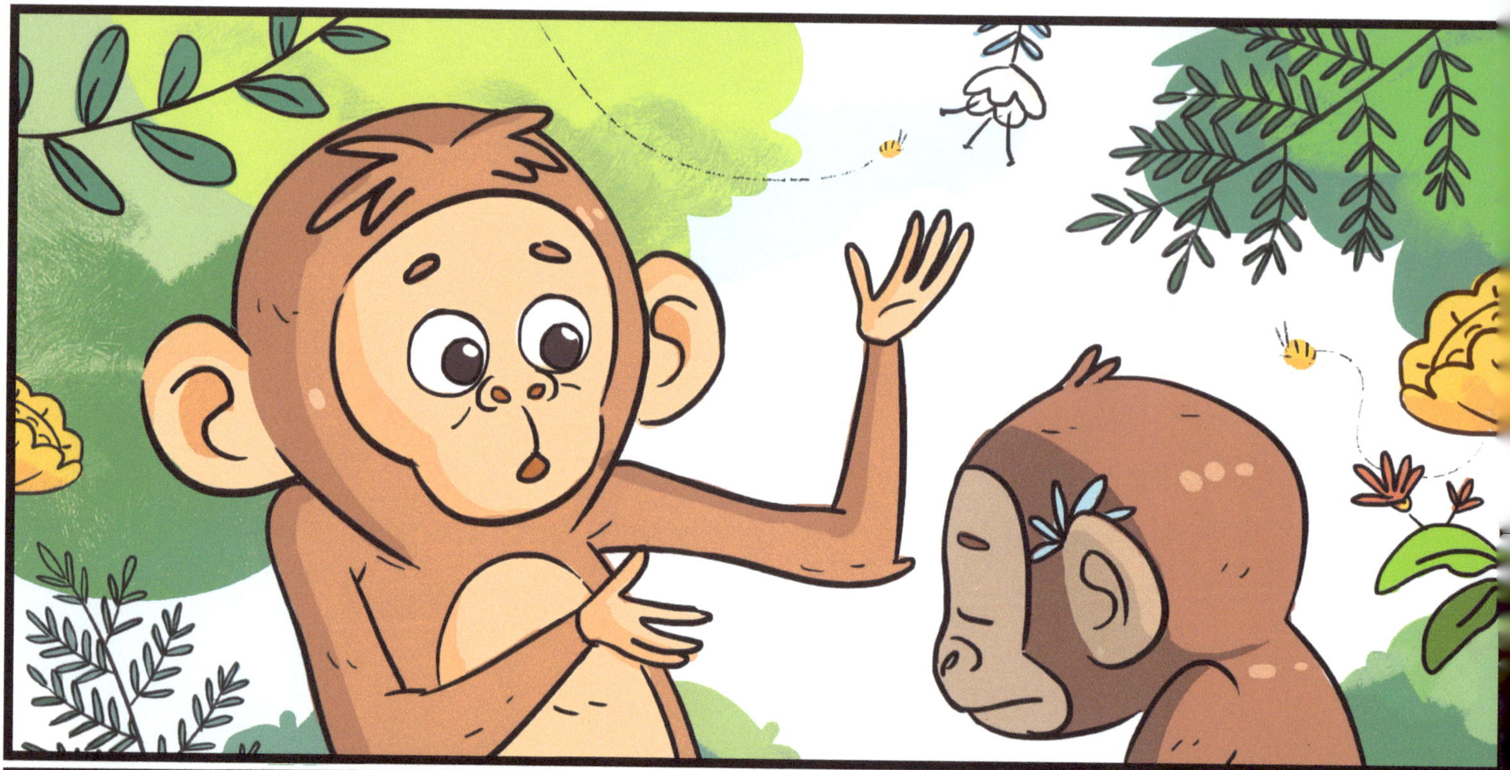

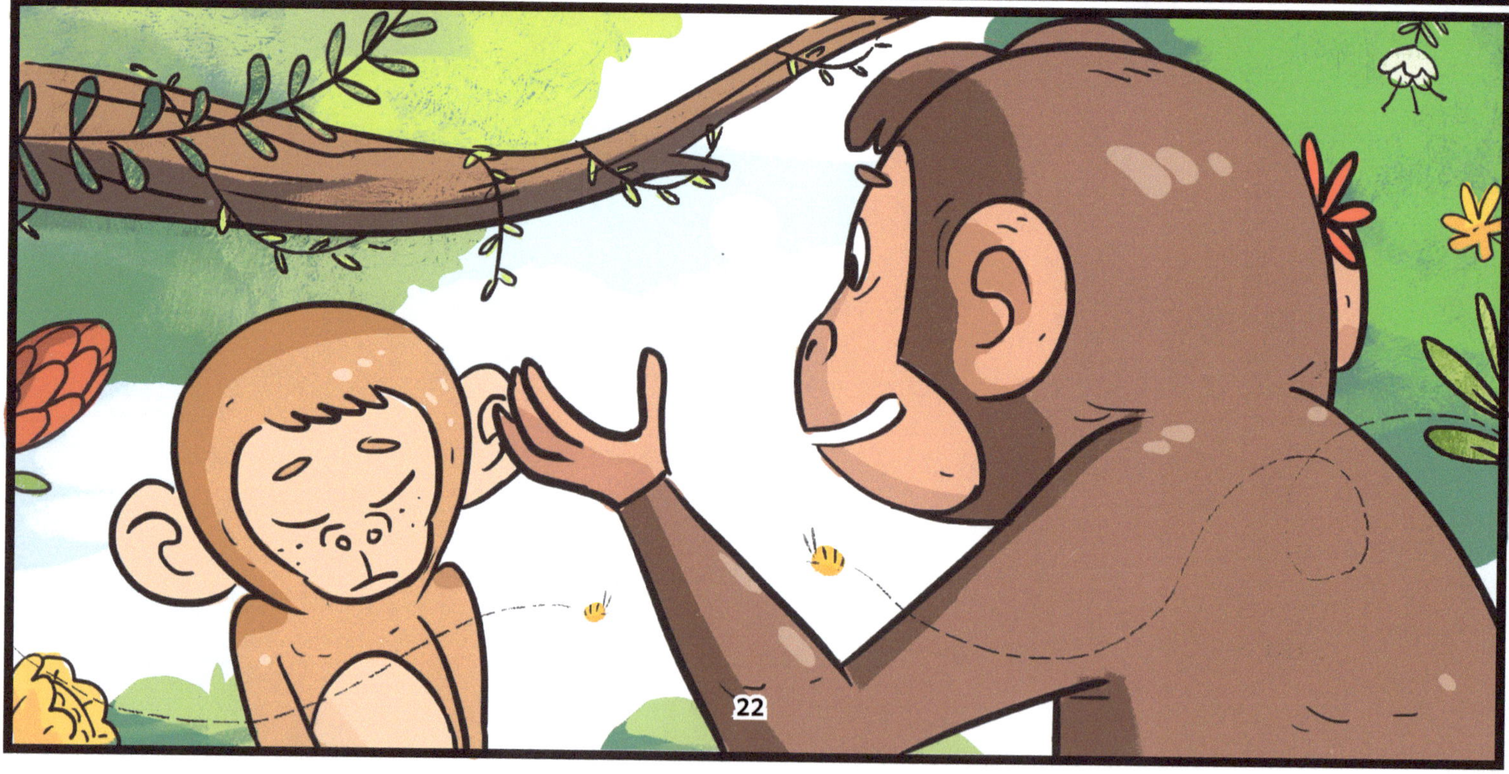

"Philly, you are not stupid. You are creative and unique.

Your umbrella helps us to drink water at night without going to the pond.

But do you see how comparing yourself

makes you sad and you feel unworthy?"

said Mommy monkey.

"No, mommy. I want to be more like Kabir and Maya.

I will use the umbrella when it rains. I want to drink orange juice from a

bottle in any season and have a cozy bed at night."

Milly sat up. "I also wish I was Maya, then I could–" Daddy said,

"Enough both of you. Remember we are–"

"Yes, I know. We are monkeys.

We eat, play, jump, and swing."

Milly sighed.

24

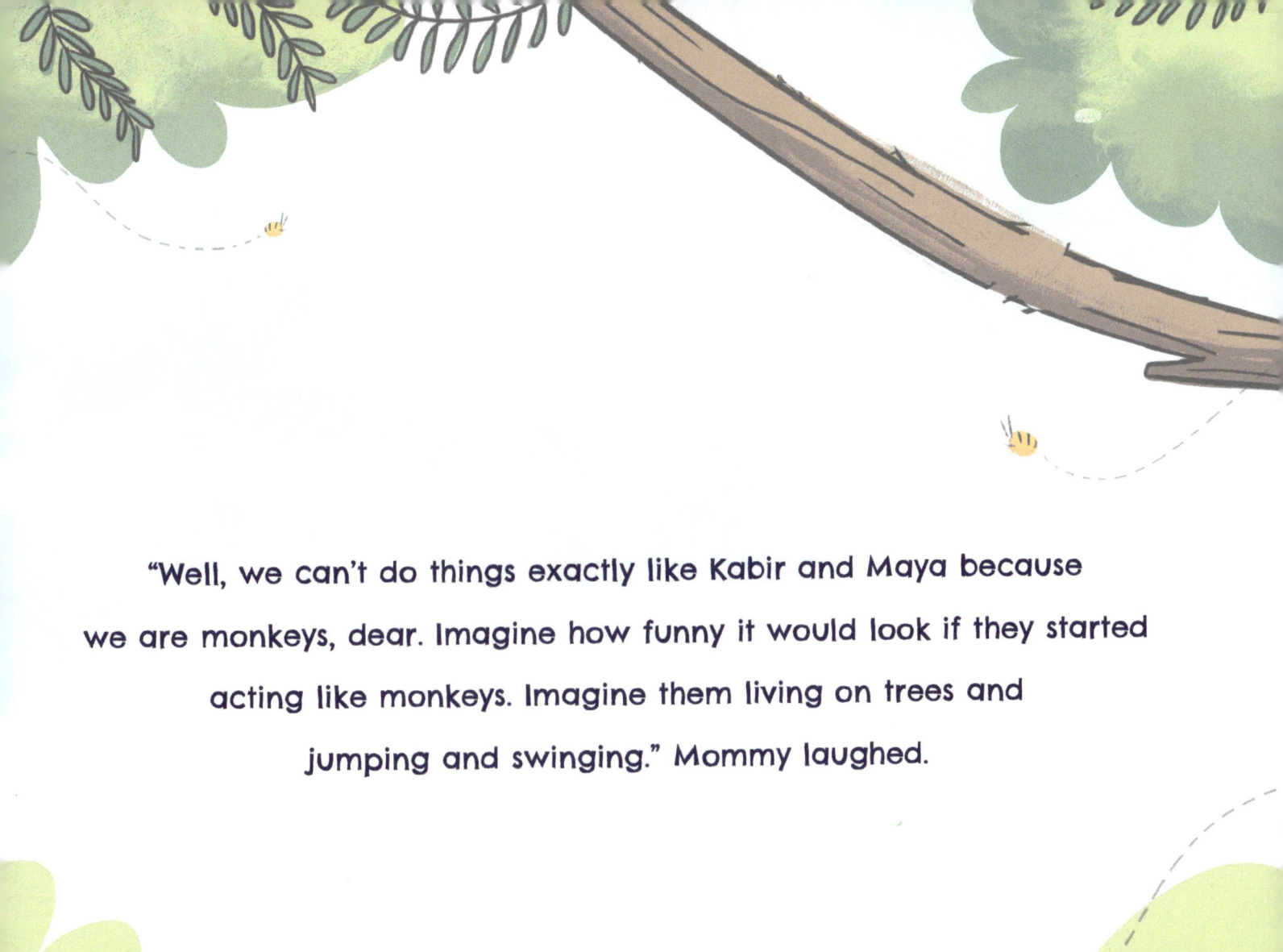

"Well, we can't do things exactly like Kabir and Maya because we are monkeys, dear. Imagine how funny it would look if they started acting like monkeys. Imagine them living on trees and jumping and swinging." Mommy laughed.

"But Kabir and Maya are cool. Why can't we live like them?" said Milly.

"Well, there is one thing we can do like them." Mommy's eyes sparkled.

"What is it?" asked Philly and Milly.

"We can go on vacation around the country, and we may also find some juicy, sweet oranges. What do you guys think?" said Mommy.

"Yes, let's do that," said Daddy.

Milly and Philly jumped up and down
and hugged each other.

28

"Daddy, what should I keep in our bags?" asked Milly.

"Nothing, dear. We don't need bags. We are monkeys,
and we are going on vacation, monkey style.
Let's get going." Mommy swung to a nearby branch.

"Noowww?" asked Philly and Milly.

"Yes, now. We can go whenever we want.
We will eat on the way," said Daddy.

So, they swung around the trees and roamed around forests and cities.

They ate oranges, mangoes, grapes, and peaches.

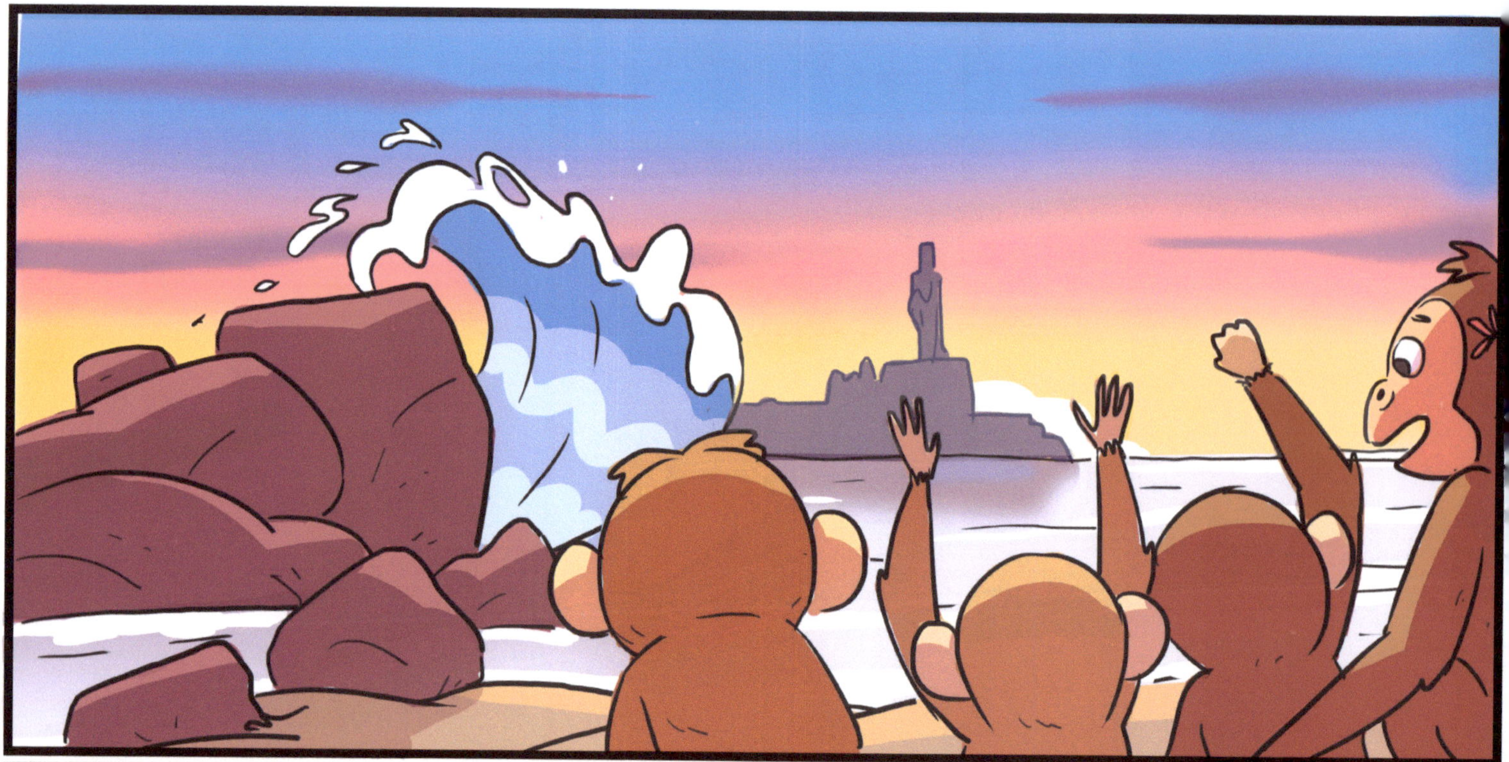

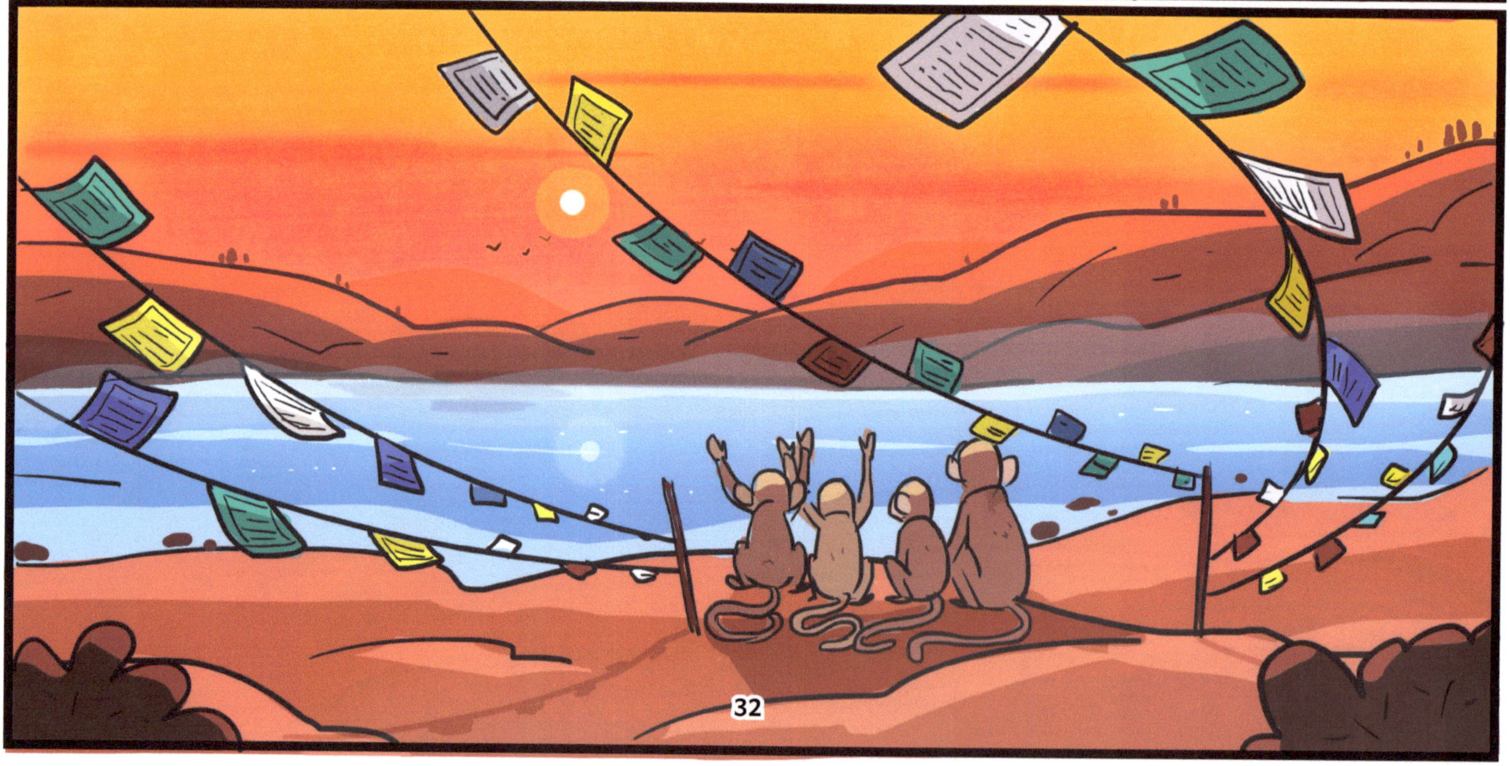

They saw a beautiful sunrise at Kanyakumari and a sunset at Pangong Tso Lake.

They enjoyed the misty hill tops of Ooty,

and the tall snow-covered pine and fir trees in Kashmir.

They learned that people spoke different languages and had diverse cultures in different regions.

At last, Daddy took them to watch the century-old ritual of Ganga Aarti,

done daily at dusk and dawn on the banks of the holy river Ganga.

Tens of thousands of people gathered to worship Ganga.

They blew conch shells, clanged brass bells, waved traditional oil lamps,

and chanted harmoniously. It was a magnificent view,

difficult to forget anytime soon.

40

When they returned home,

they met their friends and told them all about their adventures.

42

Mommy asked them,
"Do you still want to be human?
You can go on vacation for a week or two every summer then."

"Noooo!" shouted Philly and Milly together.

"We want to stay monkeys and go on vacation anytime we want,"
said Philly.

"And we love our beautiful, cozy tree home," said Milly.

Grabbing a tree branch, they swung into the air.
"And we can play, jump, and swing as much as we want."

They hugged their branches and wondered about all
the beautiful places they had seen together.

Juhi Nachane

Hello there, I'm Juhi Nachane! I spent my childhood in a quaint little town in India, where I was as mischievous as a monkey and just as silly. I started off as a curious kid who loved to explore, and somehow that curiosity led me to the world of microbiology. I stumbled into the realm of medical writing by pure accident! Life has a way of surprising us, doesn't it?

These days, I call the vibrant city of London my home, where I live with my wonderful husband and my two beautiful kids. It's funny how life takes us on unexpected journeys, right? Speaking of unexpected journeys, recently, someone asked about my dream, leaving me speechless. Strangely, that question led me here. Holding my own children's book feels like a dream itself.

Here's a secret: despite writing, talking isn't my strong suit. I've mastered late comebacks after awkward conversations, so forgive any quirky moments if we meet. Writing has always been my true voice. I truly hope you and your little ones find joy in the pages of this book. Let's embark on this reading adventure together—just promise me we won't have to chat about it!

When I'm not immersed in my artistic world, I love reading books, watching animated movies, and travelling.

www.ingramcontent.com/pod-product-compliance
Lightning Source LLC
Chambersburg PA
CBHW041433120626
46547CB00002B/203